Simple Joys

Hylain Wright

Presentation by *BookLeaf Publishing*

Web: www.bookleafpub.com

E-mail: info@bookleafpub.com

ISBN: 9789357214186

First edition 2023

I dedicate this book to my loves:

Ryan, Claudia and Emily.

ACKNOWLEDGEMENT

Thank you Bookleaf Publishing for giving me the opportunity to write and be out there in the world to be noticed.
The creation of this book is now crossed off my bucket list.

Also, a big thank you to the few people I was brave enough to tell about my participation in this writing challenge.

PREFACE

I wrote this book to challenge myself because I always wanted to write a book and be able to call myself a writer.

The short poems are rooted from life experience, literature and conversations with people throughout my life.

Childhood moments

Small footsteps upstairs
Followed by belly laughter
Tears saved for later

Bathroom

2

A place of comfort
Sensing uncanny relief
Unbearable fumes

Mushrooms

Colorful helmets
All peeking through fallen leaves
Nature's Fall army

Commuting

Peering through the glass
Mortality feels close by
Warm sunshine and shades

Nap time

Slumber on a chair
Feet propped up in comfort mode
An afternoon spent

House plants

Abundance of fresh
Friendly greetings in silence
Craving liquid care

Boardgames

Taking turns who is
Next up you throw but no dice
Victory or defeat

Soda pop

Popping out the cool
Fuzzy tongue and bubbly throat
Loud burping away

Reading journey

Escape into bliss
Or learn and marvel in awe
All through written words

Meditation

Deep breath in and out
Banish all those stressful thoughts
Pure bliss Lotus pose

Park life

Chirping in the trees
Playing and running on the grass
A picnic basket

Bath Time

My childhood story
Memories of bubbly spheres
Soapy warmth and suds

Gathering

Happy time with friends
Laughter and games oh what fun
Share food for comfort

Music and lyrics

Tap tap go my feet
Swish side to side goes my head
Bopping to the beat

Board game

We take turns each time
Will it be a lucky roll?
Victory or not?

Craftiness

Glue and paint and go
Draw abstract or realism
knit and purl cut strings

Yoga flow

Deep breath in and out
Downward dog warrior 1
Corpse pose namaste

Grocery shopping

Going down the aisle
Grabbing necessary things
Spend too much money

Video games

Press play get ready
Player one let's get going
Too late, game over

Social media

Tik Tok video
Like and react LOL
Repost and watch more

Aroma therapy

First you light the wick
Wait and then inhale deeply
Scented happiness

www.ingramcontent.com/pod-product-compliance
Lightning Source LLC
La Vergne TN
LVHW050504210726
843509LV00015BA/2995